Melva Charlene Cox Spencer

Her Life, Love, and Testimony in Poetry

Edited by Stan Spencer

FINE LIFE BOOKS

ACKNOWLEDGEMENTS

Thanks to Rita Davidson for collecting and digitizing the poems and to Rachel Sevey for the cover design.

INTRODUCTION

Melva wrote poems for many occasions and for many people; these are but a sample. I have corrected spelling, capitalization, and punctuation, and broken up long lines, but have otherwise left the poems as she wrote them, including the way she annotated and signed each one. A few poems written by George Spencer (her husband) and one by Charles Cox (her father) are also included because they are also part of her story.

Photographs on the cover of this book provide visual references for many of Melva's poems—pictures of her sister Geneva, her boyfriend-turned-husband George, his horse, their wedding, their first house, their young children, and the companionship they cherished to the end. Photographs on the front cover (left to right, top to bottom) depict Melva at age 8 and Geneva at 6 in southern Utah; Melva in Mesquite, Nevada, 1957; George riding his favorite horse, Dan, in the municipality of Buenaventura, Chihuahua, Mexico; the bride and groom on Valentine's Day, 1958, in St. George, Utah; Melva riding Rex in Buenaventura; a professional photo from the late 1970s in St. George; and George, Melva, George's sister Emma, and children Randall, Teresa, Rita, Stanley, and George in Las Vegas, Nevada. Photographs on the back cover depict Melva at 16; the dating couple playing in the Coral Pink Sand Dunes near Kanab, Utah; Geneva and Melva; Melva in her wedding dress; the two-room (kitchen, bedroom), 16-foot by 16-foot house that George built of adobe in Buenaventura the year before their wedding; the couple in a photo booth; Melva at 12, Lucy Spencer, Geneva at 10, Lily Spencer, and Harold Spencer holding dolls in Buenaventura; Melva at about 18; Melva with young George Jr., Rita, and their dog, Puppy, outside their second home in Buenaventura; the couple in church clothes in 1957, and the couple sharing a chair in about 1970.

The book is typeset simply, without headers or page numbers, for undistracted reading of the poems. The poems are divided into four sections: Parents and Siblings, Valentines, Children, and Testimony.

Parents and Siblings

Thirty Five Years

August 2, 1951

For thirty five years of married life
We have been together
My darling wife

We are just as fond of
Each other as ever, tho
We have had much to endure

We have had some pleasure
As well as sorrow in rearing
Our family of ten

Our children we have raised
In honor and taught
Them pathway from sin

Some of our going has been
Rugged and some of our trials
Were hard to bear

But we feel that we are
Living for a real purpose
And we shall always do our share

For the temptations are
Mere trifles when looking
Toward our heavenly sphere

We feel that we will have
A life far better
Than any on earth could compare

The trials and temptations
Still and many hardships
We shall have to learn

But let's not falter
In our mission here below
Be firm in our convictions
And go on forever more

—Charles C. Cox

I Loved to Hear My Daddy Sing

Dedicated to my father, Charles Chester Cox, May 2002

Oh I had a dear Daddy
Who was as sweet as he could be.
So many songs he sang to me
As I sat upon his knee.

He was patient and kind in manner
A gentle man in deed.
So tender with our mother
And anyone in need.

I had a little sister
Who sat on his other knee.
And with our arms around his neck
Our love for him was plain to see.

When outside it was cold and stormy
And all the chores were done
We would climb upon our Daddy's knee
And then our fun began.

He sang to us from the hymn book
And songs both sweet and sad
Songs of a serious nature
But most to make us glad.

We loved to hear his tenor voice
And feel his love and care.
Oh how happy were those evenings
When his singing filled the air.

Oh how I loved to hear my Daddy sing
In those sweet days gone by.
And now he sings the angels' songs
In that lovely place on high.

—*Melva C. C. Spencer*

Joyous Reunion

I remember playing in the garden
When I was a little girl.
They tell me I was a sweetheart
With my hair in golden curls.

I played with my sisters dear.
I counted as blessings all five of them.
My brothers, too, were special to me.
Oh how I long to see them each again.

My daddy was strong, gentle, and kind;
My mother the sweetest ever.
Our home was happy and full of joy.
We wanted always to be together.

As time passed and changed our lives
We each went our separate ways.
But reunions brought us close each year.
How we looked forward to those days.

Now we dwell in eternity
And are scattered here and there.
May we be reunited once again
Is my constant pleading prayer.

—*Melva Charlene Cox Spencer*

Boring Evening

*We would come to St. George and stay in a house we had
rented Saturday night so we could attend church the next day.
My sister's boyfriend, Delmer, would come and stay very late.
I had to sleep in the living room on the couch so I couldn't go
to bed until he went home.*

Boring evening
Nothing to do
I'm tired of the talk
Of all of you

There's nothing to read
That interests me
And my eyes are so heavy
I can hardly see

I'm hungry and tired
I've starved all day
When I come to town
It's always this way

The loves in a swoon
Keep me up all night
I can't go to bed
Without kicking up a fight

For the places I sleep
Are the places they are in
And laughter and talk
Are a noisy din

When finally this morning
I got to bed
My soul was so weary
And a pain in my head

I tried to sleep
I turned and tossed
Rolled and groaned
'Til consciousness I lost

And at sunup or rising
With a heavy head
My bones ached with sleeping
On a hard old bed

I went to church
With my mind in a daze
And tried to learn
Of God's holy ways

And now this evening
It's the same old thing
I wish our company
Would be on the wing

I guess I sound rude
And selfish too
But I'm so tired
I don't know what to do

—*Melva Cox*

Home Country

I gaze down on home country with my eyes
and my heart registers so many mixed emotions.
Feelings of pain and sweetness swell my mind—
the love in a good home
the closeness, companionships
the good times
the beautiful singing of a father
deep concern of a mother
extreme closeness of brothers and sisters—
but again, the pain
the loneliness, the poverty, the rejection
the deep longing for friends, acceptance—
so many mixed emotions.
I tingle to go there
to breathe of the sweet night air
the freshness uncontested
to gaze at the vast sky overhead
to smell the desert flowers
to feel that sweet at-home feeling
but the painful memories come again
and my feelings are repulsed.
So I go there in my memories
and for short visits in person
but too many days have I spent there in suffering
to stay for long.
That, mixed with the sweetness
of pungent memories of loved ones
leave it a place of mental emotions, forever.

—*MCCS*

This Warm Comforter

A note given on quilts to two of my sisters, Velda and Zella, for Christmas 1985

Use this warm comforter
On a cold and frosty morn
While you stoke up the heater
To keep you toasty warm

—*Melva C. C. Spencer*

A Colorful Quilt
Put on a quilt I made for my sister Zella

I'm just a colorful quilt
Made especially for you
Now to make me very happy
This is what you do

Put me on the back
Of your favorite chair
Wrap me around you
And keep out that cold air

And when you bow your head
To take a little nap
I'll keep you warm and cozy
Can I be better than that?

—Melva C. C. Spencer

My Parents

Written to my parents, Charles and Retta Cox, Jan. 1986

I could feel it—
The closeness
The something down deep
Quiet, calm within.
No words could express
Nor were needed.
He entered the room
Stooped, gave her a kiss.
"How's my sweetheart?"
He said.
She smiled, answered briefly
Went on with her
Mending.
He picked up a book
Settled into a chair
After a moment
Began to read aloud.
With a tilt of her head
She listened
Content, companionship.

After many years striving together—
Family, failures, success
Sorrow, pain, and tears
Joy and fulfillment—
Now slowed with the weight of years
Life gave them a gift
Of faithfulness, understanding
Love, joy within, complete.
A successful marriage
Was this.

—*Melva C. C. Spencer*

Side by Side with My Mother

To my mother, Retta Stock Cox

Sometimes I long to see her
And to sit by her side once more
To feel of her love and friendship
As I did in days of yore.

I wonder how it will feel once again
To embrace her and see her face.
How does she look after all this time
Having dwelt in a much better place?

Will the lines and the pain be gone?
Will she be serene and at peace?
Did she step forward with a joyful heart
Once her trials on earth did cease?

A righteous woman was she
Though her life was long and hard.
She made the world a better place
By her faithfulness in doing her part.

My mother how well I remember
The comfort you brought each day
As we depended on your love and shoulder
To help us go on our way—

The hours you spent in our service
The deep concern you had for each one
How you cared for and directed
From the day each life began.

Someday we'll meet again, Mother
And once more sit side by side
And will share our feelings once more
Up there in peace, where you now abide.

—*Melva Charlene Cox Spencer*

My Sister, My Friend

Written to my sweet sister, Geneva Cox Tanner, January 2002

We grew up together
Side by side
Close to the same age
And the very same size

We were friends deep down
Always and ever
We understood each other
And squabbled never

She was my best friend
We were pals hand in hand
In friendship and sisterhood
We would forever stand

We played in the garden
And climbed the tall trees
Ran in the meadow
Safe, happy and free

We played with our dolls
And with love understood
The pleasure of life
And sweet motherhood

When growing up together
We shared our joys
And friendships with others
The girls and the boys

We both chose good men
To marry that would live
With examples of great manhood
Our children to give

As we grew older, we each
Went our separate way
But only in distance
Our friendship would stay

That friendship that
Began in Heaven above
Would remain strong in our hearts
Forever in sisterly love

—*Melva Charlene Cox Spencer*

That Sweet Sister of Mine

May 2002, to my sweet sister Rita V. C. Cox

Oh there is a jewel of priceless treasure
It's someone sweet and sublime
She is an earthly angel
That sweet sister of mine

The soft rays of sun in the meadow
And flowers that bloom in springtime
Are not any more beautiful
Than that sweet sister of mine

Her heart is soft and tender
Her actions are always kind
Her goodness is forever
That sweet sister of mine

The singing of birds in the treetops
Singing in time and in rhyme
Are still not as beautiful
As that sweet sister of mine

—Melva C. C. Spencer

Valentines

Wishing Ring

1953, written to my boyfriend, George

If I had a wishing ring
I know what I would do
I would turn it on my finger
And send a wish to you

I'd wish you all the happiness
With joy, and peace of mind
I'd wish you wishes that would bring
Pleasures of all kind

And though I don't have the ring
To wish them all for you
I'd wish them anyway
Hoping they'll come true

—*Melva Cox*

Precious Things

To Melva, July 22, 1953

Precious things are hard to find
And far apart that's true
But of all the precious things
The one I love most is you

—*George W. Spencer*

A Note to Say Goodbye

To my boyfriend, George W. Spencer

This is just a note to say goodbye
Before I leave, you know
To tell that I love you
Once again before I go

I shall surely miss the Sundays
When we read and talk and play
Yes, I will surely miss you
Every single day

—*Melva Cox*

My Darling Melva

Written several years before we were married

My Darling you are leaving
But my heart is going too.
Just keep it with you darling.
Always let my heart go along with you.

But when you return dear
Let my heart come back with you
Because with you is where I want it.
I love you very much darling I do.

—George W. Spencer

Goodbye

To my boyfriend, George, 1953

I don't like to say goodbye
For it makes me want to cry.
Others will see my tears you know.
That's why I don't want you to go.

—*Melva C. Cox*

Stars

To Melva, July 30, 1953

Of all the stars I've ever seen
The ones I'd rather see
Are the ones that sparkle in your eyes
When you look at me

—*George W. Spencer*

Tears at Parting

To my boyfriend, George, 1953

There's always tears at parting
With the ones we love the best.
For the ones with whom we're parting
Are dearer than all the rest.

We never know their value
Until we're forced to part.
When we bid goodbye the last time
'Tis wringing on the heart.

—Melva C. Cox

You Are the One

August 3, 1953

You are the one I dream about
And the one I'm thinking of
But some day you will find out
You are the one I truly love

That I am in love with you
And that love is deep you see
That you are so good and sweet
You are always in my memory.

The while that you all were here
Was a great time but ended much too soon.
Wow the time I'm dreaming of
Is me and you under a big full moon.

—*George W. Spencer*

To the One I Love

Written to Melva before they were married

I am lonesome but yet I'm happy
Thinking of you my love
Wishing you the most of happiness
And God's blessings from above

I feel so very lonesome my Dear
I miss you so very much
I want you with me always
I enjoy the tenderness of your touch

I think very much of you Darling
I love you! You are swell
I will try to always make you happy
And always keep you well

I appreciate your love and kindness
Tis more than I deserve
I will try and not disappoint you
With a greater effort my Father I will serve

I know I am weak my Darling
But with your help and love
I will seek to gain salvation
That we may live in peace above

We must seek for life eternal
The commands of our Father to obey
And so live to see our Maker
At the great and final day

So Darling will you help me
Give me a lift when I am down
And may we share Celestial glory
And inherit a throne and a crown

These are my wishes Darling
Will you and can you understand
And forgive and help me always
Help me to become a man

—*George W. Spencer*

He Rode Upon a Beautiful Stallion

To George W. Spencer

He rode upon a beautiful stallion
One look at him and I knew
That one day in the future
I would say "I do"

A handsome face
With a teasing grin
A blond head under a cowboy hat
On a frame strong and thin

With feet in the stirrup
He turned and galloped away
With a wave of his hand and a promising smile
That he would soon return my way

As we rode together over hill and dale
And through the country side
Somehow deep within us each we knew
That someday I would be his bride

Then distance came between us
As we went our separate ways
Though letters flowed between us
Those were the lonely days

After five long years of waiting
We knelt together at the altar
And exchanged our vows
To be together now and forever

—*Melva Charlene Cox Spencer*

My New Husband

To my husband, George W. Spencer

He took my hand; we were one
Together we walk a new road
Alone together
A home to build and furnish with love
Cleave unto each other
Is the counsel from above

I touch his shoulder
Broad, strong, and youthful
Strong, straight and true he is
And spiritual
We kneeled together
This day at a sacred altar

Vow's we promised each other
Before witnesses and Heavenly Father
He counseled us, leave father and mother
And build happiness together

It's hard cutting strong bonds
From home and family
Like taking a bird from a nest
And trying brand new wings

It's using the strength
And wisdom we learned at home
To build new hope and life
And walk together hand in hand
As man and wife

It's new loyalty to new life
It's trying and crying and caring
Walking away from the old
Into the new

Only can we make a life together
If we love each other
Enough to strive together
And leave behind our childhood homes

—*Melva C. C. Spencer*

In Our Honeymoon Car

In our shiny Chevy honeymoon car
We drove south to Chihuahua, Old Mexico
What was at the end of that rough dusty road
I did not really know

We moved into our first new home
Made of adobes—mud and sand
Built by my honey the year before
Away down in this faraway land

It was a small two-room cabin
With two windows and one outside door
With warm brown walls within it
And a cold cement floor

But we did not need a castle
To make a happy home
We did not need silver or gold
Or to sit upon a throne

We hung curtains in the windows
And threw rugs upon the floor
Put pictures on the bare brown walls
And a welcome on the door

It only took our happy hearts
From the day that we were one
To fill the rooms of our adobe hut
With laughter, love and song

No, it did not take a castle
To fill our hearts with joy
And we added even more beauty
With a beautiful girl and a fun-loving boy

Yes, we made our two-room cabin
A castle of frolic and fun
With our beautiful little baby girl
And our handsome playful son

—*Melva C. C. Spencer*

Everything to Me

Written to my husband, George W. Spencer

I don't think there could ever be
Another man like you
No other sweet and tender one
With heart so good and true

No other man who could
Be quite so heavenly
And radiate the warm romance
That is a part of me

There never could be someone else
Who is to me a king
Because my dear your very presence
Makes life so serene

Your good looks go much deeper
Than all outward looks embrace
The beauty of your inner self
Outshines your form or face

No other one, no other one
Could ever, ever be
For you are everything my love
Everything to me

—Melva Charlene Cox Spencer

Jorge

To my husband on Father's day

Just to live in the warmth and love of your care
And heaven is on earth, to know when I need you,
    you're there
It's contentment to be by your side thru this life
And to know that forever I'll be your wife

My love Forever, Melva

My Husband

Dedicated to my husband, George W. Spencer

He's my husband
He seems so strong to me
A good front, a calm face
Quiet nature, a gentle race
My protector, a gentle hand
And broad shoulders to lean on
The strength of him
Brings security to my life
And yet I know
Nothing can destroy manhood
Quicker than a wife
He needs my support
My loyalty and love
He needs gentle words
And warm embraces
So he can face a world
Of hardness and challenge
He needs my gentle touch
My faith, my belief in him
For I know he is perishable and tender
And sensitive within

This I know, and my love
Will build of him a great man
Where my carelessness
And criticism would destroy him
So help me God to be a wife
To build a love divine
To make my home a haven
A place of refuge for him
My own, my love, my life

—Melva C. C. Spencer

George Sr.

I'm trying to think
Of some tricky rhyme
But time is passing
And there just isn't time

So I guess this little note
Will have to do
That you're my sweetheart
And my hero, and I love you

—*Melva Charlene Cox Spencer*

To My Love, Jorge

October 20, 1984

You're there
Breathing softly in deep sleep
The warmth of you
Creeps softly across the sheet
And warms my soul
With the sense of security
You're there
Next to me, my love, my life
A deep sense of peace and contentment
Fill my heart
You are
The roses in my life
And the sweet perfume of happiness
Is my companion
The thorns
Of my life
Are when you're not there

Forever, Melva

—Melva C. C. Spencer

To my Love, George

July 17, 1990

In this hectic life we live
The rush, rush, rush
The hurry, hurry, hurry
The work, work, work
And the people, people, people
The constant ringing of the
Phone and the doorbell
The coming and going
And then at the end of the day
When the clutter
Is cleared away
And the dust is settled
You're there my friend
My companion
My security
My everything
To relax with you my love
Makes my life worth while
And wonderful
May we share many more
Of your birthdays together

Forever yours, Melva

—Melva Charlene Cox Spencer

To My Honey, George

February 14, 2000

42 years ago we shared
Our first kiss over the altar
(Well, it was our first kiss over the altar)
But since then, we've always been together

Side by side, arm in arm
For many a footstep in life's run
My darling, my friend, my husband
Life has been good, life has been fun

You've sheltered me, protected me
Always been near, always been there
Always together whatever the reason
Bowed our heads in sorrow and bowed them in prayer

Rejoiced together in the good times
That far outnumber the bad
Found joy in a wonderful family
In each precious lass, each wonderful lad

With the light of the gospel to guide us
A living prophet to show us the way
The Savior, our Redeemer to love us
And to hear whenever we pray

Could life really be more wonderful?
I can't think of a way that it could
For with you forever beside me
It will always be wonderful and will always be good

Your wife forever, Melva

—*Melva C. C. Spencer*

The Light in My Window

To My Honey, George, September 2003

The sun that shines in the morning
Is the smile upon your face
It's the sweet kiss you give me
As you hold me in warm embrace

When moonlight shines through the window
And puts a halo round your hair
No words need be spoken
As we contently linger there

Let me lay my head on your shoulder
And feel your arms around me
Hold me close sweetheart forever
Forever close to thee

As we walk through the meadows
Over life's hills and dale
With you forever beside me
My joy will never fail

You're the light in my life and my window
Through which joy and contentment shine
Forever you'll be mine, my darling
And forever I will be thine

—*Melva C. C. Spencer*

Fifty Years of Love

To my Sweetheart, George, January 2008

What a surprise, would you look at that
Who is that riding up in a cowboy hat?
He tipped it at an angle on a handsome head
And with a smile on his face, "Hello," he said

He dismounted his horse and held out his hand
A gentleman he was in a foreign land
My heart gave a leap and I could feel the beat
This was a young man I was happy to meet

We rode horses together to mountains far and near
With him to protect me I had no fear
We walked side by side and hand in hand
I had met some before, but this was the man

We knelt by the alter and exchanged our wedding vows
We cherished each other then, but even more now
50 years ago this man that I loved
Is still my precious gift from heaven above!

My love forever, Melva

—Melva C. C. Spencer

Wishing Ring

To George W. Spencer

If I had a wishing ring
I'd make a wish you see
I'd wish that I could talk to you
And you could talk to me

I'd tell you all the news I know
And listen while yours, you told
And sing the songs with you again
As in days of old

—Melva Cox

Children

Waiting

Written while waiting in the doctor's office for my 6th, 7th, or 8th

Waiting for the doctor—what a joy!
Wondering what it's going to be, a girl or a boy
The same old things to do, the same old time to wait—
How much longer is the real date?

Some new person's birthday
That's what it's all about.
It seems forever, but it will happen
Even though there's doubt.

The wait is long and tiresome
And don't forget the pain.
And when it's all over
We do it all again.

For the joy of holding a new one
A tiny precious soul
Until you're a mother
You'll never really know.

The joy that comes from creation
The joy of giving birth
To Heavenly Father's children
And bringing them to earth.

But waiting for the doctor
Is really not a joy
And I am still wondering
Is it a girl or a boy?

—*Melva Cox Charlene Spencer*

Four Little Girls

Four little girls and four little boys
Have come down one by one
From Heavenly Father's mansions
To bless our little home.
And what a great joy each little one
Has brought into our hearts.

—*Melva C. C. Spencer*

Two Small Shoes

To my son Derek, age 6

In the middle of the room
In the center of the floor
Or in the hallway
Or not far from the door—

Always two small shoes.
Every single time
He enters the house
That small son of mine—

He kicks them off
And lets them settle
Wherever they choose.
And there's no need to meddle—

He just doesn't remember
Or it slips out one ear
It doesn't sink in
Or he doesn't even hear.

For no matter what I say
Or what my reminders
There's his two small shoes
Just where they were before.

But as I bend to pick them up
And love makes my heart warm
I like seeing those two small shoes—
I wouldn't wish them any harm.

I love the small boy they fit
And though he never remembers where they go
I'm glad to see these two small shoes
For the boy they fit—I love him so.

—*Melva Charlene Cox Spencer*

Fishing

Summer of 1985

I see another Mother
Sitting in the car, waiting
Reading and waiting patiently
For her menfolk to fish.
Fishing down in the brook
Is pure delight for boys
And dads when boys are eleven
Like Derek—fishing is fun.
And they would rather fish than eat
And that's saying a lot.
Beautiful here in the mountains
Cloudy overhead and a stillness
On the water in the dam.
Just across the road
These tall pines slowly
Moving in a whispered breeze
Refreshing and cool, just right
For fishing and thinking, yes
Just right for boys and dads
To fish in complete contentment.

And just right for mothers
And wives to wait and read
And write sitting in the car
On a soft seat.
Getting sleepy, remembering
The hard bed last night
In the tent, bake-oven dinner
A little overdone but perfect.
What could go wrong
In this mountain atmosphere?
Unless Derek doesn't
Catch any fish!

—*Melva C. C. Spencer*

Cleaning the Spare Room

April 2003

I'm cleaning out the spare room
If there is something I can spare.
I'll keep the desk—it was my mother's.
And I love this antique chair.

The closet is full of clothes
All of them just hanging there.
Which of these things must go?
Which of them can I spare?

No, not the little scout shirt—
It walks softly on my heart
And reminds me of a dear young lad.
No, I cannot with it part.

That flowing gown, that beautiful dress
For my daughter so sweet and fair—
It brought a warmth within my breast.
No, it must keep hanging there.

And all of these games and toys
My little ones used to play.
I see their joy and happiness—
They will have to wait another day.

I think I'll just walk out of here
And come back some other day.
This spare room with lots to spare
That I cannot spare today.

—*Melva C. C. Spencer*

My Posterity, My Prayer

May 2006

Bless them to walk in thy ways, dear God.
Keep their hands close in thine.
Guide them in thought and act, please God
That their lives may with righteousness shine.

Oh please, dear God, don't let them stray
From the truth, and joy of thy ways.
Keep them close in thy heart and mind
That joy and success may fill their days.

Bless them to love, serve, and to care
To be kind to their fellow men.
Bless them to pray and forever seek thee
That each may live with thee once again.

Each of these, my posterity, dear God—
My love for each is strong and warm.
I pray with my heart and soul, dear God
Oh, keep them safe from evil's harm.

Walk by their side, lift them forever up
Strengthen them in each desire and will.
Oh please, dear God give them courage to live
And each their missions on earth to fulfill.

—Melva C. C. Spencer

My Children, My Valentines

George Jr.—
One tall, dark
Special son
Determined to do right—
I'm proud of you.
One clean, wholesome
Son
Honest and truthful—
I'm proud to say
You're mine.
One studious and
Determined to succeed—
I'm proud to
Call you "Son."

Rita—
That pretty smile
And dark shining hair
Clear, honest eyes
And a personality
Of pure sweetness
Compassion and
Sincerity
Make one beautiful
Girl, "my daughter."
I'm proud to call
You my
Sweet valentine.

Teresa—
Golden hair
Just like an
Angel
That you are
Dedicated to right
And sincere
With sweetness
That matches
Your smile.
You're mine and
I'm happy and
Proud, my daughter
Valentine

Stanley—
Dependable
Sincere, good-
Natured and
Honest; a ray
Of sunshine
And quiet joy—
You bring contentment
To my heart
My son, and I'm
Proud and content
Valentine

Randall—
A heart full of song
A joy to hear and
See. You, my son
Are special in so
Many way—your
Loyalty to family
Friends and faith—
I'm proud of you.
To share life
With you is joy
My son and
Valentine

Cynthia—
One sweet girl
So full of fun
Such a joy to have
To love and hold
Such fun to
Share your
Work and play—
I'm so proud of you
Every single day
My daughter
My valentine

Marcia—
A bubbly bundle
Of fun
Always on the go
Always on the run
A sweet
Smile and happy
Voice—you're the
Sunshine in my
Life and my love
Little valentine

Derek—
Live it up
Always on the go
Making hearts
Beat happier
A ray of sunshine
Adding so much
Fun to every day—
My two year old
My little son
My valentine

Testimony

My Mia Maids

Written for my Mia Maid girls, 1980

The beauty of
Roses
And beauty of
Girls
With sweet
Perfume
And feminine
Curls

Each to bloom
Forever
With sweetness of
Soul
Forever for
God—
May this be your
Goal

—*Melva Cox Charlene Spencer*

A Guiding Book Mark

I am only a book mark
I have no beauty or charm
But if you will my instructions
They will keep from you evil and harm

Put me in your scriptures
So you will always know
When you read them each day
Just the right page to go

Drop to your knees often
Plead with God above
To guide your footsteps each day
And feel of His strength and love

Plead for the Holy Spirit
To be your guiding light
That each day no matter what
You will always do what's right

Keep the Sabbath day holy
And honor your covenants, each one
That you will be ready to meet Him
When again our Savior does come

Look to the prophet for counsel
Listen to his every word
Follow these instructions my dear
And walk with joy your life's road

—*Melva C. C. Spencer*

March Forward in Peace

July 2002

I will go before you, saith the Father
And I will be your rearward.
I will protect you, counsel, and direct you
If you will obey and keep my word.

I will also be in your midst
And the power of heaven shall come
To assist, protect, and sustain my saints
That I may gather each of them home.

Diligently teach thy children of the Lord
And great shall be thy peace.
Terror and fear shall depart from thee
If thy prayers unto God never cease.

No weapon against thee shall prosper
And evil tongues shall not succeed.
Your heritage shall be greatly blessed.
My strength shall support you in your need.

Go forward my saints—march forever forward
In the cause of truth, of light, and love.
Teach my gospel, put on a righteous armor.
Trust in the strength and guidance from above.

—*Melva Charlene Cox Spencer*

The Temple Beautiful

2002; grandfather Isaiah Cox worked on the St. George temple

I gaze up with awe at the temple
A house of our Father and God
A beautiful enlightened house of peace
Of Jesus Christ our Lord.

Standing white, tall and stately
Reaching high into heaven's light
With soft rays coming downward
To enlighten all who enter inside.

A place of refuge for my soul
Where the Spirit comes strong and clear
A place of peace and answered prayer
As I enter with those I hold dear.

My grandfather's strong hands
Callused from years of hard toil
Worked to build this Holy House
Of our God on sacred soil.

Built by the hands of the priesthood
Of God so many years ago—
I feel his love and concern for us
Though him we did not know.

Did he think of the years ahead
As he labored with care and skill
And pray for us his descendants
To enter there and obey God's will?

Thank you my dear grandfather
For your testimony and for your love
For your commitment and hard labor
And for your concern from above.

May we forever honor your name
And remember your service and care.
As your descendants may we live
To someday greet and dwell with you there.

—*Melva C. C. Spencer*

A Lonely Chair

She leaned back in her reclining chair
A dreamy far away look in her eyes.
Tiny tears rolled down her cheeks.
She softly whispered, "How quickly time flies."

With quick eager steps, she walked in life
Answering requests of those in need
With warm, holding arms and shoulders soft
Tender-hearted with love in every deed.

Now she sits alone and drifts away
To those happy days now gone.
Her thoughts go back to loved ones and friends
And her home filled with happy song.

Her doorbell is painfully silent
Her phone so long between rings.
How she longs for the companionship and joy
That someone on her doorstep could bring.

Could someone return a gift of love
That she through her life has given?
Could someone cheer up a lonely heart
And give a dear soul just a bit of heaven?

Will we someday sit in a reclining chair
With our thoughts drifting far away
And long for a visit, a touch and a hug
From a friend in a hurried busy day?

—*Melva C. C. Spencer*

I Need Your Help Today

September 2005

Dear God
I need the Holy Ghost
To be with me each day.
I know if I get angry
It will quickly go away.
So please, Dear God
I need Your help today.

When bad thoughts
Come into my mind
And I let them stay.
The Spirit will go quickly.
Please, Dear God
I need Your help today.

If I find fault with another
Or speak in an unkind way
I know the Spirit will depart.
Please, Dear God
I need Your help today.

When I feel all upset
And argue to get my way
I know it isn't right, Dear God
I need Your help today.

Please help me walk uprightly
And have charity within.
Help me to love my neighbor.
Keep me free from sin.

I know if I am worthy
To be under the Spirit's shielding arm
It will give me guidance and comfort
And protect me from evil and harm.

I need the constant companionship
Of the sweet and guiding light.
I need Your help each day, Dear God
That I may do what's right.

Please help me keep the Holy Ghost
To always guide my way.
Please bless me with strength, Dear God.
I need Your help each day.

—*Melva C.C. Spencer*

My Savior, My Brother

He will take me in His arms again
And call me by my name.
And the love I felt so long ago
Will feel the same again.

That brother-sister friendship
So deep, so sweet and pure
Through a long separation
Will forever more endure.

My Savior, my Brother, my Redeemer
My Guiding Light, my Best Friend—
With a constant plan for me to follow
His caring and concern has no end.

He was my Friend before earth time.
I listened as He taught the way
And my heart cries out in yearning
To be with Him again someday.

—*Melva C. C. Spencer*

My Best Friend and I

My best friend and I
Had a visit one day.
He counseled and blessed me
Before I went on my way.

He talked to me softly
With love in his voice.
And blessed me to always
Make the right choice.

Then he bid me farewell
And did softly say
Return to me with honor
On a beautiful day.

—*Melva C. C. Spencer*

www.ingramcontent.com/pod-product-compliance
Lightning Source LLC
Chambersburg PA
CBHW070833100426
42813CB00003B/600